INTRODUCTION

For almost 50 years much of the world believed that German soldiers had massacred upwards of 10,000 Polish officers during March and April 1940 at a forest in Poland called Katyn. This in spite of official German denial and an international forensic study that left no doubt that the killings were the work of the Soviet Union. Because of the war then going on (in 1943) the Allies were willing to overlook the German evidence contained in this booklet and were eager to believe Soviet denials. In the postwar world people should have questioned Soviet denials and examined the German evidence, but many did not. Only with the collapse of the communist regime in the Soviet Union was the truth of this 1943 German report to be confirmed.

The account that follows is a direct translation from the original German text of this booklet, which was published by the German government in 1943 in an effort to present the German point of view regarding the massacre. No attempt has been made in the translation to edit out the anti-Jewish elements found in the original German text. Rather, they have been left in to preserve the original historical context of the document.

THE MASS-MURDER IN THE KATYN FOREST
A DOCUMENTARY ACCOUNT OF EVIDENCE

For years little or nothing was known of the fate of the Polish divisions that had fled to the east at the end of September 1939 after the sudden collapse of the Polish Army. There was no doubt that they were captured by the invading Bolsheviks. It was said that the Polish officers and men had been separated and that most were being held in huge camps.

Inquiries as to their fate from the "Polish Government-in-Exile" in London were met by Soviet silence. When Polish representatives in Moscow requested permission to visit the prisoner-of-war camps they were arrested for espionage. This in spite of the fact that Mr. Sikorski, head of the Polish delegation, had offered to assemble a Polish Army for service with the Soviets in their war with Germany.

Gradually it became known that those Polish troops that had not been released or killed had been forced into the Soviet Army. The fate of their officers however, was unknown. They had disappeared without a trace, as if the earth had opened up and swallowed them. Much later it became dreadfully clear that that is almost what happened to them.

During the summer of 1942, Polish troops were attached to the German Army in the vicinity of Smolensk. Rumors circulating among the local population reported that in 1940 several transport trains of Polish officers had been unloaded by the Soviets at the railway station in Gniesdowa. The officers were trucked to a nearby forest where they were shot. The Polish troops investigating the rumors found graves containing human remains but had no idea of the extent of the horror in the Katyn forest. When the German unit to which the Polish troops were attached moved out of the area, the matter was dropped. The local population was sufficiently frightened and intimidated by the long period of horror during the Bolshevik occupation, that they would not openly discuss the events of 1940 with German authorities. It was not until the spring of 1943 that the Germans learned of the graves in Katyn forest.

The Germans committed the energy and resources needed to get to the facts of what had happened. Excavations and eyewitness accounts soon painted a ghastly picture of mass murder that surpassed all human imagination: along a row of hills in a grave that varied from 15 to 30 yards wide and up to 4 yards deep were the bodies of approximately 12,000 Polish officers laid one on top of another, up to 12 deep. Without exception, each had been executed by the infamous Soviet bullet in the neck at the base of the skull. Katyn forest had finally yielded its secret. The fate of the Polish officers was now horribly clear.

The general public in Germany is to be given adequate information about the nature of these large-scale mass murders carried out on the orders of Soviet-Jewish officials. While we will limit what we say about this matter the photos and documents that follow will speak for themselves in all their horror.

People in neutral foreign countries have been paralyzed with horror by news of the Soviet slaughter as it began to be published by German authorities. Katyn became the symbol of Bolshevism. Those in Moscow who conceived of the murders, and their allies in England and the United States were dumbfounded for some time after publication of the facts. Then, as expected a flood of lukewarm denials and counter accusations were released. Obviously, the allies said "the Fascists [Nazis] committed the mass shootings themselves" only to blame the Soviets for them.

The incontestable conclusions of a group of international authorities of forensic medicine that the bloody murders had to have been committed more than 12 months prior to any German soldier entering the area, does not seem to bother the Jews in Moscow, London and Washington. In the same breath with the angry allied counter accusations they have reported that the Katyn forest site is an archeological excavation of a prehistoric burial ground! One is expected to believe that the classic Soviet liquidation technique of a bullet fired into the base of the skull, has been around for a thousand or more years.

So many accusations, so many lies - and not a single one of them is even clever. If proof of the capital crimes of the Soviet murderers and their useless denials of them was needed, it was provided by the unanimous verdict of the team of international forensic specialists who examined the crime scene. Because of its objectivity this verdict is one of the most disturbing known to humanity. With the entire world looking on it brings a conclusion to the drama that took place in the forest of Katyn in the early months of 1940. The verdict is:

Smolensk, 30 April 1943

TRANSCRIPT

Recorded as a conclusion of the examination of mass graves of Polish officers in the forest of Katyn near Smolensk by leading representatives of European forensic medicine and criminology schools and other renowned university professors.

From 28 to 30 April 1943 a commission composed of leading representatives of European forensic medicine and criminology schools and other renowned medical university professors conducted a scientific examination of the mass graves of Polish officers in the forest of Katyn near Smolensk.

The commission consisted of the following gentlemen:
1) Belgium: Dr. Spelers, Professor of Opthamology an the University of Gent.
2) Bulgaria: Dr. Markov, Forensic Medicine and Criminology teacher at the University of Sofia.
3) Denmark: Dr. Tramsen, Prosector at the Institute of Forensic Medicine in Copenhagen.
4) Finland: Dr. Saxén, Professor of Pathological Anatomy at the University of Helsinki.
5) Italy: Dr. Palmieri, Professor of Forensic Medicine and Criminology at the University of Naples.
6) Croatia: Dr. Miloslavich, Professor of Forensic Medicine and Criminology at the University of Agram.
7) Netherlands: Dr. de Burlet, Professor of Anatomy at the University of Groningen.
8) Protectorate of Bohemia and Moravia: Dr. Hájek, Professor of Forensic Medicine and Criminology in Prague.
9) Rumania: Dr. Birkle, Forensic Doctor of the Rumanian Ministry of Justice and first assistant at the Forensic Medicine and Criminology Institute in Bucharest.
10) Switzerland: Dr. Naville, Professor of Forensic Medicine at the University of Geneva.
11) Slovakia: Dr. Subik, Professor of Pathological Anatomy at the University of Bratislava and Slovakian Chief of State Public Health Works.
12) Hungary: Dr. Orsós, Professor of Forensic Medicine and Criminology at the University of Budapest.

Also present during the inspection and deliberations were
1. Dr. Buhtz, Professor of Forensic Medicine and Criminology at the University of Breslau. He was authorized by General Headquarters of the German Army to be in charge of the excavations in Katyn.
2. Dr. Costedoat, Medical Inspector, ordered to be present during the inspection of the Commission by the head of the French Government.

The discovery of mass graves of Polish officers in the forest at Katyn near Smolensk that was recently brought to the attention of German authorities has caused Dr. Conti, the State Health Leader, to invite the above mentioned specialists from several European countries to come to Katyn to examine the site and help with the clarification of this unique case.

The Commission personally interviewed a few local Russian eyewitnesses who confirmed that in the months of March and April 1940 large railway transports of Polish officers were unloaded almost daily at the Gniesdowa railway station near Katyn. The officers were then transported to the Katyn forest by trucks and were never seen again. The commission also took further notice of previous discoveries and determinations and examined the recovered evidence. By 30 April 1943, 982 corpses had been exhumed. Of those, about 70% were immediately identified while the papers of the others will be utilized for identification only after a careful pretreatment. The corpses that were dug up prior to the arrival of the Commission were viewed as a group and autopsies were performed by Professor Buhtz and his co-workers on the majority of them. Seven mass graves were opened up of which the largest contained an estimated 2500 bodies. The members of the Commission personally performed autopsies on nine corpses while many specially chosen corpses were submitted to a coroners inquest.

<u>Forensic conclusions of the completed reviews and examinations.</u>

The cause of death of all the exhumed corpses is without exception a shot in the head. Mostly single shots in the nape of the neck, but in a few cases double shots. In one instance there were three shots in the nape of the neck of the corpse. The entry wound is typically located at the nape of the neck and leads through the bone of the back of the skull and into the cavity in which the spine terminates. The exit wound is usually in the area of the forehead/hairline. All victims were killed by pistol shots of a caliber of under 8 mm.

As a result of the explosion of the skulls, the residue of burned powder in the area of the entry wound, and the similar locations of the entry wounds it is concluded that the victims were shot at point blank range. The direction of the shot is the same, with only a few exceptions. The noticeable similarity of the wounds within a very limited region on the back of the skull shows a practiced hand. On many corpses the hands were bound in a standard way, and in a few cases bayonet wounds in clothing and skin were noted.

Corpses of Russian civilians that were also exhumed in the forest of Katyn had their hands bound like those of the Polish officers, even though the Russians were buried much earlier. It was concluded that the Russian civilians were also shot in the nape of the neck by a steady, practiced hand. In one instance a Polish officer that had already been killed by a neck shot was subsequently hit by a bullet that had killed another officer. Only the outer bone surface was damaged by the bullet. This probably proves that the shootings actually took place in the open graves, thereby eliminating the necessity of transportation to the graves.

The mass graves are located in clearings in the forest and have been completely obliterated by flattening the earth and planting small young pine trees. The Commission members themselves and a statement from a hired consultant, Chief Forester von Herff, concluded that the pine trees were a maximum of five years old, were poorly developed because of the shade and were probably planted at this spot about three years ago. The mass graves are laid out like steps in the hilly sandy land. They reach ground water in some places.

Nearly all corpses were found laying in the prone position, very close together or overlapping each other. Towards the ends they are clearly arranged while in the center the arrangement is more irregular. In nearly all cases the legs are stretched out. The arrangement is obviously systematic. The entire Commission agreed that the exhumed corpses were dressed in clothing that

Translation is continued inside back cover.

DER MASSENMORD
im Walde von Katyn

Ein Tatsachenbericht auf Grund amtlicher Unterlagen

Über das Schicksal der polnischen Divisionen, die nach dem raschen Zusammenbruch der polnischen Wehrmacht Ende September 1939 nach Osten geflüchtet und von den einrückenden Bolschewisten gefangengesetzt worden waren, herrschte jahrelang völlige Unklarheit. Nur soviel war bekannt geworden, daß das Gros der polnischen Truppen in mehreren großen Lagern untergebracht war, Offiziere und Mannschaften streng voneinander getrennt. Allen Nachfragen der polnischen „Emigranten-Regierung" in London setzten die Sowjets eisiges Schweigen entgegen, alle Versuche der polnischen „Vertretung in Moskau", die Gefangenenlager aufzusuchen, wurden auch dann noch mit Verhaftungen wegen Spionage beantwortet, als der Krieg zwischen Deutschland und der Sowjetunion längst ausgebrochen war und der „Ministerpräsident" der polnischen Emigration, Sikorski, als willfährige Kreatur Londons dem Kreml die Aufstellung einer polnischen Armee in sowjetischen Diensten anbot.

Allmählich wurde bekannt, daß ein Teil der Mannschaften, soweit sie nicht bereits umgekommen waren, freigelassen, ein anderer in sowjetische Dienste gepreßt worden sei. Das Schicksal der polnischen Offiziere aber war nach wie vor in undurchdringliches Dunkel gehüllt. Sie blieben unauffindbar, als habe die Erde sie verschluckt. Wie nahe dieser Vergleich der Wirklichkeit kommt, sollte man erst viel später mit gräßlicher Deutlichkeit erfahren . . .

Im Sommer 1942 kamen einige Polen im deutschen Wehrmachtgefolge in die Nähe von Smolensk. Gerüchtweise erfuhren sie von der einheimischen Bevölkerung, auf dem Bahnhof Gniesdowa seien wiederholt Transporte mit gefangenen polnischen Offizieren angekommen, die dann in Lastwagen abtransportiert und in dem nahen Walde erschossen worden seien. Die Polen gingen dem Schicksal ihrer Landsleute nach und stießen beim Graben tatsächlich auf Leichen polnischer Offiziere. Auf welch grauenhaftes Massengrab sie gestoßen waren, scheinen sie aber nicht geahnt zu haben. Da die deutsche Einheit, der sie sich angeschlossen hatten, bald darauf abrückte, ließen sie die Sache auf sich beruhen. Die Bevölkerung, völlig eingeschüchtert und verängstigt durch die bolschewistische Schreckensherrschaft der vergangenen Jahre, hatte bisher nicht gewagt, über ihre Erlebnisse im Jahre 1940 zu sprechen. So verging ein weiteres Jahr, bis im Frühjahr 1943 die ersten Mitteilungen über Leichengruben im Walde von Katyn zu den Ohren der deutschen Behörden gelangten. Energisch und systematisch werden sofort alle Mittel eingesetzt, den Fall aufzuklären. Grabungen und Zeugenvernehmungen ergeben nach kurzer Zeit ein so grauenhaftes Bild des Massenmordes, daß es alles menschliche Vorstellungsvermögen weit überschreitet: In einer Reihe von Hügeln mit einer Ausdehnung von durchweg 15 × 30 m bis zu einer Tiefe von 4 m liegen, dicht zusammengepreßt, oft in 12 Schichten übereinander, die Leichen von rund 12 000 polnischen Offizieren — ausnahmslos durch den berüchtigten Genickschuß der GPU ermordet. Der Wald von Katyn hat sein Geheimnis preisgegeben, das spurlose Verschwinden der polnischen Offiziere seine entsetzliche Aufklärung gefunden.

Die deutsche Öffentlichkeit ist über die Einzelheiten dieses größten, unter dem Kommando jüdischer GPU-Funktionäre durchgeführten Massenmordes ausreichend unterrichtet worden. Wir können uns daher darauf beschränken, die Bilder und Dokumente der nachstehenden Seiten in ihrer ganzen Furchtbarkeit für sich sprechen zu lassen.

Die Reaktion auf die deutschen Veröffentlichungen ist im neutralen Ausland lähmendes Entsetzen über die Untat der GPU-Schlächter; Katyn wird zum Fanal des Bolschewismus schlechthin. Den intellektuellen Urhebern der Morde in Moskau und ihren Verbündeten in England und in USA verschlägt es tagelang den Atem. Dann aber bricht, wie zu erwarten, eine Flut sich überschlagender Dementis und Beschuldigungen los: Selbstverständlich sind die den Sowjets in die Schuhe geschobenen Massenerschießungen „von den Faschisten selbst begangen worden". Daß nach den einwandfreien Feststellungen zahlreicher internationaler Autoritäten der gerichtlichen Medizin die Morde mindestens 12 Monate vorher begangen sein müssen, ehe ein deutscher Soldat die Gegend der ungeheuerlichen Bluttat betrat, ficht die Juden in Moskau, London und Washington nicht im geringsten an. In einem Atem mit diesen wütenden Gegenbeschuldigungen wird behauptet, es handle sich bei Katyn — um die archäologische Ausgrabungsstätte eines frühgeschichtlichen Gräberfeldes! Als ob man schon vor tausend und mehr Jahren das bewährte sowjetische Liquidierungsmittel des Genickschusses gekannt hätte. Soviel Behauptungen, soviel Lügen — und nicht einmal geschickte!

Wenn es noch eines Beweises für die Blutschuld der sowjetischen Massenmörder und für die Sinnlosigkeit ihrer Dementis bedurft hätte, so lieferte ihn das gemeinschaftliche Gutachten der internationalen gerichtsmedizinischen Sachverständigen, die den Tatort besuchten und untersuchten. Dies Gutachten ist trotz oder gerade wegen seiner Sachlichkeit eines der erschütterndsten Dokumente, das die Menschheitsgeschichte kennt. Es setzt vor der Weltöffentlichkeit den Schlußpunkt hinter das Drama, das sich in den ersten Monaten des Jahres 1940 im Walde von Katyn abspielte. Das Gutachten lautet:

z.Zt. Smolensk, den 30.April 1943

P R O T O K O L L

aufgenommen anläßlich der Untersuchung von Massengräbern polnischer Offiziere im Walde von Katyn bei Smolensk, die durch eine Kommission führender Vertreter der Gerichtlichen Medizin und Kriminalistik europäischer Hochschulen und anderer namhafter medizinischer Hochschullehrer durchgeführt wurde.
In der Zeit vom 28. bis 30.4.1943 hat eine Kommission führender Vertreter der Gerichtlichen Medizin und Kriminalistik europäischer Hochschulen und anderer namhafter medizinischer Hochschullehrer die Massengräber polnischer Offiziere im Walde von Katyn bei Smolensk einer eingehenden wissenschaftlichen Untersuchung unterzogen.
Die Kommission bestand aus folgenden Herren:

1. Belgien:	Dr. S p e l e e r s, ord. Professor der Augenheilkunde an der Universität Gent,
2. Bulgarien:	Dr. M a r k o v, ord. Dozent für gerichtliche Medizin und Kriminalistik an der Universität Sofia,
3. Dänemark:	Dr. T r a m s e n , Prosektor am Institut für gerichtliche Medizin in Kopenhagen,
4. Finnland:	Dr. S a x é n, ord. Professor der pathologischen Anatomie an der Universität in Helsinki,

5.	Italien:	Dr. P a l m i e r i, ord. Professor der gerichtlichen Medizin und Kriminalistik an der Universität Neapel,
6.	Kroatien:	Dr. M i l o s l a v i c h, ord. Professor der gerichtlichen Medizin und Kriminalistik an der Universität Agram,
7.	Niederlande:	Dr. d e B u r l e t, ord. Professor der Anatomie an der Universität in Groningen,
8.	Protektorat Böhmen u. Mähren:	Dr. H á j e k, ord. Professor der gerichtlichen Medizin und Kriminalistik in Prag,
9.	Rumänien:	Dr. B i r k l e, Gerichtsarzt des rumänischen Justizministeriums und erster Assistent am Institut für gerichtliche Medizin und Kriminalistik in Bukarest,
10.	Schweiz:	Dr. N a v i l l e, ord. Professor der gerichtlichen Medizin an der Universität Genf,
11.	Slowakei:	Dr. Š u b i k, ord. Professor der pathologischen Anatomie an der Universität in Preßburg, Chef des Staatlichen Gesundheitswesens der Slowakei,
12.	Ungarn:	Dr. O r s ó s, ord. Professor der gerichtlichen Medizin und Kriminalistik an der Universität Budapest.

Bei den Arbeiten und Beratungen der Delegation waren ferner anwesend:

1. der vom Oberkommando der Deutschen Wehrmacht mit der Leitung der Ausgrabungen in Katyn beauftragte ord. Professor der gerichtlichen Medizin und Kriminalistik an der Universität Breslau, Dr. B u h t z,
2. Médecin-inspecteur Dr. C o s t e d o a t, der vom Chef der französischen Regierung beauftragt worden war, den Arbeiten der Kommission beizuwohnen.

Die vor kurzem zur Kenntnis der deutschen Behörden gekommene Entdeckung von Massengräbern polnischer Offiziere im Walde von Katyn bei Smolensk hat den Reichsgesundheitsführer Dr. Conti dazu veranlaßt, die obengenannten Fachgelehrten aus verschiedenen europäischen Ländern zur Besichtigung der Fundstelle nach Katyn einzuladen, um zur Klärung dieses einzigartigen Falles beizutragen.

Die Kommission vernahm persönlich einige russische einheimische Zeugen, die u. a. bestätigten, daß in den Monaten März und April 1940 fast täglich größere Eisenbahntransporte mit polnischen Offizieren auf dem nahe bei Katyn gelegenen Bahnhof G n i e s d o w a ausgeladen, in Gefangenenautos nach dem Wald von Katyn transportiert, später nie wieder gesehen wurden; sie nahm ferner Kenntnis von den bisherigen Befunden und Feststellungen und besichtigte die aufgefundenen Beweisstücke. Hiernach sind bis zum 30.4.1943 982 Leichen ausgegraben worden. Davon wurden etwa 70 Prozent sofort identifiziert, während die Papiere der übrigen erst nach sorgfältiger Vorbehandlung zur Identifizierung verwertet werden können. Die vor dem Eintreffen der Kommission ausgegrabenen Leichen sind

sämtlich besichtigt, in größerer Zahl auch obduziert worden, und zwar durch Professor Buhtz und seine Mitarbeiter. Bis zum heutigen Tage wurden 7 Massengräber eröffnet, deren größtes schätzungsweise 2500 Offiziersleichen enthält.
Von den Mitgliedern der Kommission wurden persönlich 9 Leichen obduziert und zahlreiche, besonders ausgewählte Fälle einer Leichenschau unterzogen.

Gerichtlich-medizinische Ergebnisse der durchgeführten Besichtigungen und Untersuchungen.

Als Todesursache der sämtlich bisher ausgegrabenen Leichen wurde ausnahmslos Kopfschuß festgestellt. Es handelt sich durchweg um Genickschüsse, und zwar überwiegend um einfache Genickschüsse, in seltenen Fällen um doppelte Genickschüsse, in einem einzigen Fall um einen dreifachen Genickschuß. Der Einschuß sitzt durchweg tief im Genick und führt in den Knochen des Hinterhauptsbeins nahe am Hinterhauptsloch hinein, während der Ausschuß in der Regel in der Gegend der Stirn-Haargrenze, in ganz seltenen Fällen tiefer liegt. Es handelt sich durchweg um Pistolenschüsse von einem Kaliber von unter 8 mm.
Aus der Sprengung des Schädels und dem Befund von Pulverschmauch am Hinterhauptsknochen in der Nähe des Einschusses sowie aus der gleichartigen Lokalisierung der Einschüsse ist auf Schuß mit aufgesetzter Mündung oder aus unmittelbarster Nähe zu schließen, zumal auch die Richtung des Schußkanals mit wenigen geringen Abweichungen durchweg gleichartig ist. Die auffallende Gleichartigkeit der Verletzungen und der Lokalisation des Einschusses in einem ganz be-

schränkten Bereich der Hinterhauptgegend lassen auf eine geübte Hand schließen. Bei zahlreichen Leichen konnten gleichartige Fesselungen der Hände und in einigen Fällen auch 4-strahlige Bajonettstiche an Kleidung und Haut festgestellt werden. Die Ausführung der Fesselung entspricht den an Leichen russischer Zivilisten festgestellten Fesselungen, die ebenfalls im Walde von Katyn ausgegraben und schon viel früher begraben wurden. Es wurde ferner festgestellt, daß auch die Genickschüsse bei den Leichen von Zivilrussen ähnlich zielsicher abgegeben wurden.

Aus der Feststellung eines Querschlägers im Kopfe eines durch Genickschuß getöteten polnischen Offiziers, der nur die äußere Knochentafel eingedrückt hatte, ist zu schließen, daß durch dieses Geschoß erst ein anderer Offizier getötet worden ist, und daß es nach Austritt aus dessen Körper in die Leiche eines bereits erschossen in der Grube Liegenden eingedrungen ist. Diese Tatsache läßt vermuten, daß Erschießungen offenbar auch in den Gruben stattfanden, um einen Transport zur Grabstätte zu vermeiden.

Die Massengräber befinden sich in Waldlichtungen. Sie sind vollkommen geebnet und mit jungen Kiefernbäumchen bepflanzt. Nach dem eigenen Augenschein der Kommissionsmitglieder und der Aussage des als Sachverständigen zugezogenen Forstmeisters von H e r f f handelt es sich um wenigstens 5jährige, im Schatten großer Bäume schlecht entwickelte Kiefernpflanzen, die vor 3 Jahren an diese Stelle gepflanzt wurden.

Die Massengräber sind stufenförmig in das hügelige Gelände, das aus reinem Sand besteht, vorgetrieben. Sie reichen zum Teil bis ins Grundwasser.

Die Leichen liegen fast ausschließlich in Bauchlage dicht neben- und übereinander, an den Seiten deutlich geschichtet, in der Mitte mehr unregelmäßig. Die Beine sind fast immer gestreckt. Es handelt sich offensichtlich um eine systematische Lagerung. Die Uniformen der ausgegrabenen Leichen haben nach übereinstimmender Wahrnehmung der Kommission sämtlich im Ganzen und Einzelnen, insbesondere in Bezug auf Knöpfe, Dienstrangabzeichen, Auszeichnungen, Stiefelformen, Wäschestempel usw. die eindeutigen Kennzeichen polnischer Uniformen. Es handelt sich um Winterbekleidung; häufig finden sich Pelze, Lederjacken, Strickwesten, Offiziersstiefel, typische polnische Offiziersmützen. Nur bei ganz wenigen Leichen handelt es sich nicht um Offiziere, in einem Fall um einen Geistlichen. Die Maße der Kleidung entsprechen den Maßen der einzelnen Körper. Die Unterkleidung ist ordnungsmäßig zugeknöpft, Hosenträger, Gürtel ordnungsmäßig angebracht. Daraus ergibt sich, daß die Leichen in den von ihnen bis zum Tode getragenen Uniformen verscharrt wurden.

Bei den Leichen befinden sich keine Uhren und Ringe, obwohl Uhren nach den mit genauen Zeitangaben versehenen Aufzeichnungen verschiedener Tagebücher bis in die letzten Tage und Stunden hinein vorhanden gewesen sein müssen. Edelmetallgegenstände wurden nur in verborgener Lage bei ganz wenigen Leichen entdeckt. Dagegen fanden sich bei vielen Leichen noch Goldzähne im Gebiß. Polnische Banknoten wurden in größeren Mengen vorgefunden, in nicht seltenen Fällen auch Wechselgeld. Ferner fanden sich polnische Zigaretten- und Streichholzschachteln bei den Toten, in einigen Fällen auch Tabakdosen und Zigarettenspitzen mit der Gravierung „Kocielsk“ (Namen des letzten sowjetischen Gefangenenlagers der meisten Ermordeten). Die bei den Leichen vorgefundenen Dokumente (Tagebücher, Briefschaften, Zeitungen) stammen aus der Zeit von Herbst 1939 bis März und April 1940. Das letzte bisher festgestellte Datum ist das einer russischen Zeitung vom 22.4.1940.

Es finden sich verschiedene Grade und Formen der Verwesung, die durch die Lagerung der Leichen innerhalb der Grube und zueinander bedingt sind. Neben Mumifizierung an der Oberfläche und an den Rändern der Leichenmasse findet sich feuchte Mazeration in den mittleren Teilen der Leichenmasse. Die Verklebung und Verlötung der benachbarten Leichen durch eingedickte Leichensäfte, insbesondere die durch die Pressung bedingten korrespondierenden Deformationen weisen entschieden auf primäre Lagerung hin.

Es fehlen gänzlich an den Leichen Insekten und Insektenreste, die aus der Zeit der Einscharrung stammen könnten. Hieraus ergibt sich, daß die Erschießungen und die Einscharrungen in einer kalten, insektenfreien Jahreszeit geschehen sein müssen.

Eine größere Reihe von Schädeln wurden auf eine Veränderung untersucht, die nach Erfahrungen von Professor Orsós zur Bestimmung der Zeit des Todes von großer Wichtigkeit ist. Es handelt sich hierbei um eine kalktuffartige mehrschichtige Inkrustation an der Oberfläche des schon lehmartig homogenisierten Gehirnbreies. Solche Erscheinungen sind bei Leichen, die weniger als 3 Jahre im Grabe gelegen haben, nicht zu beobachten. Ein derartiger Zustand fand sich u.a. in einer sehr ausgeprägten Form im Schädel der Leiche Nr.526, die an der Oberfläche eines großen Massengrabes geborgen wurde.

Zusammenfassendes Gutachten:

Im Walde von Katyn wurden von der Kommission Massengräber von polnischen Offizieren untersucht, von denen bisher 7 geöffnet sind. Aus diesen wurden bisher 982 Leichen geborgen, untersucht, zum Teil obduziert und schon zu 70 Prozent identifiziert.

Die Leichen wiesen als Todesursache ausschließlich Genickschüsse auf. Aus den Zeugenaussagen, den bei den Leichen aufgefundenen Briefschaften, Tagebüchern, Zeitungen usw. ergibt sich, daß die Erschießungen in den Monaten März und April 1940 stattgefunden haben. Hiermit stehen in völliger Übereinstimmung die im Protokoll geschilderten Befunde an den Massengräbern und den einzelnen Leichen der polnischen Offiziere.

(Dr.Speleers) (Dr. Markov) (Dr. Tramsen) (Dr.Saxén)

(Dr.Palmieri) (Dr.Milosavich) (Dr.de Burlet) (Dr.Hájek)

(Dr.Birkle) (Dr.Naville) (Dr.Šubik) (Dr.Orsós)

Das Kapitel Katyn ist abgeschlossen. Es wird weiterleben als der größte und brutalste Massenmord der Weltgeschichte, und ist doch nur ein, wenn auch besonders schauerlicher Fall jüdisch-bolschewistischer Mordpraxis. Was aber als Sache der gesamten europäischen Kulturwelt weitergeht, ist der Kampf gegen ein System, das den Massenmord zum Mittel seiner Politik erhoben hat. Die Opfer von Katyn vereinigen sich mit den Opfern aus Litauen, Lettland und Estland, mit den Millionen Menschen, die der Bolschewismus in seiner 25jährigen Blutherrschaft auf sein Gewissen geladen hat. Sie verlangen klare Entscheidung von jedem verantwortungsbewußten Europäer. Katyn ist das furchtbare Schulbeispiel dafür, was der Bolschewismus mit stillschweigender Unterstützung Englands und Amerikas aus Europa machen würde, wenn es ihm und seinen jüdischen Henkern gelänge, nach Westen vorzudringen und Europas Kulturländer zu überschwemmen. Wenn das geschähe, hieße das Massengrab von morgen nicht mehr Katyn, sondern Europa.

F. R.

In der Nähe von Smolensk liegt der Schauplatz des grauenhaftesten Mordes der Weltgeschichte: Rund 12 000 polnische Offiziere wurden hier von den Henkern der GPU viehisch hingeschlachtet

Hier liegen sie, die stummen Zeugen bolschewistischer Mordlust, eine furchtbare Anklage gegen die Henker der GPU und die sowjetische Regierung

In mühevoller Arbeit wurde Grab für Grab freigelegt. Bis zu 4 m Tiefe waren die Leichen der ermordeten Offiziere eingegraben

Eine halb freigelegte Grube, die herausstehenden Schädel zeigen deutlich, daß die Ermordeten in vielen Schichten übereinander lagen

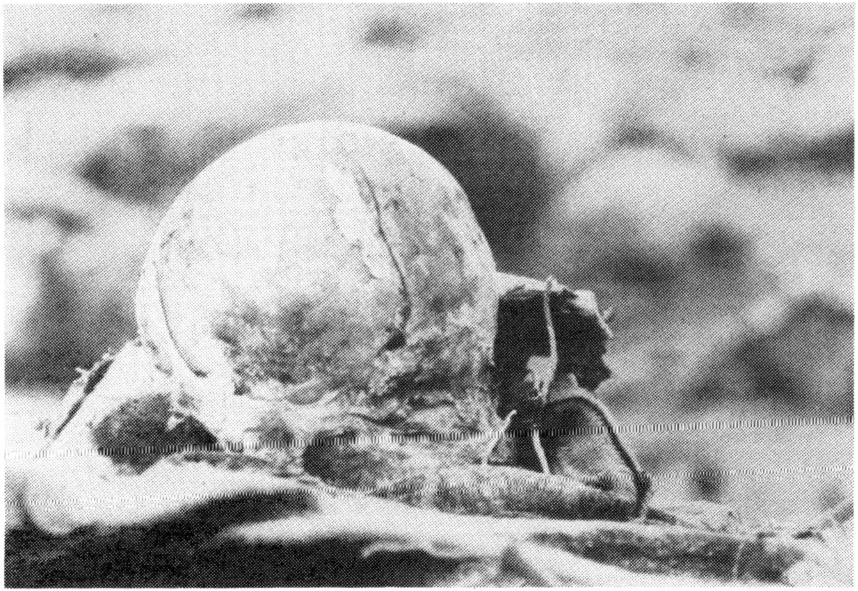

Dieser Schädel läßt deutlich den Genickschuß erkennen, dem alle Offiziere zum Opfer fielen

In mehreren Reihen übereinandergeschichtet wurden die Opfer gefunden

In den Massengräbern von Katyn ist der Welt ein schauriger Beweis bolschewistischer „Menschheitsbeglückung“ gegeben worden

In zahlreichen Gruben, deren Länge durchweg 15 × 30 m beträgt, haben die Henker der GPU ihre Opfer verscharrt

Diese freigelegten Leichen sind ein erschütterndes Dokument bolschewistischer Vertiertheit

Während manche Leichenreihen genau nebeneinander lagen, haben die GPU-Schlächter andere Opfer in wirrem Durcheinander in die Gruben geworfen

Ein gräßlicher Anblick: Mit gefesselten Händen, den Kopf mit einem Sack verbunden, fand man diese Leiche in einer der Mordgruben

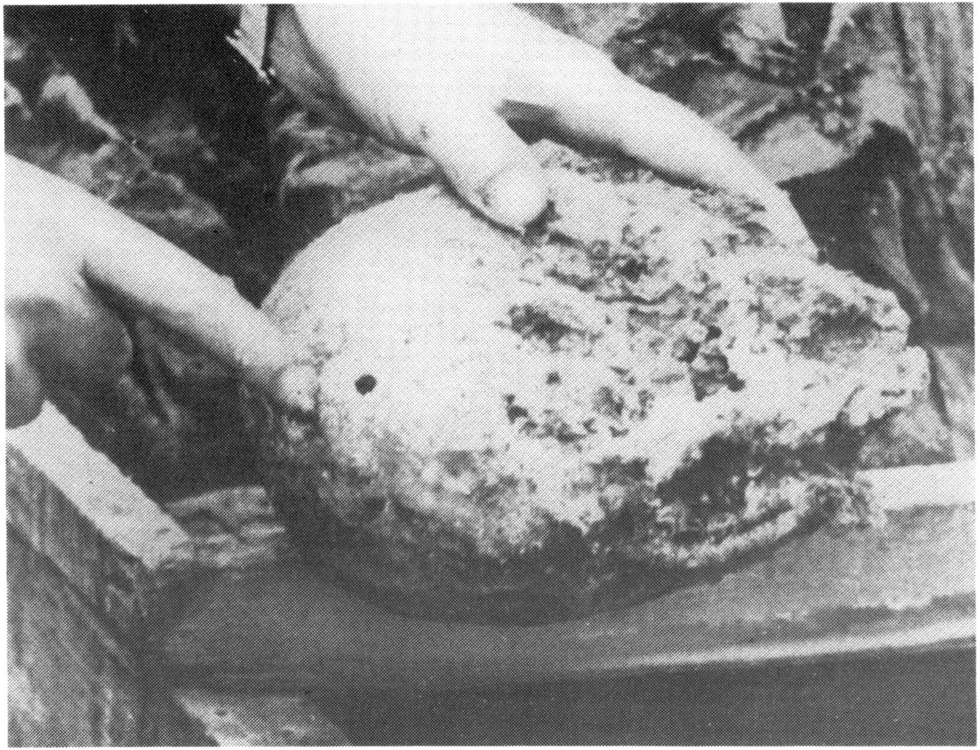

Die Todesschüsse wurden aus geringster Entfernung **abgegeben**: Die meisten **Schädel zeigen** außer dem Einschuß im Genick auch einen Ausschuß an der Schädeldecke

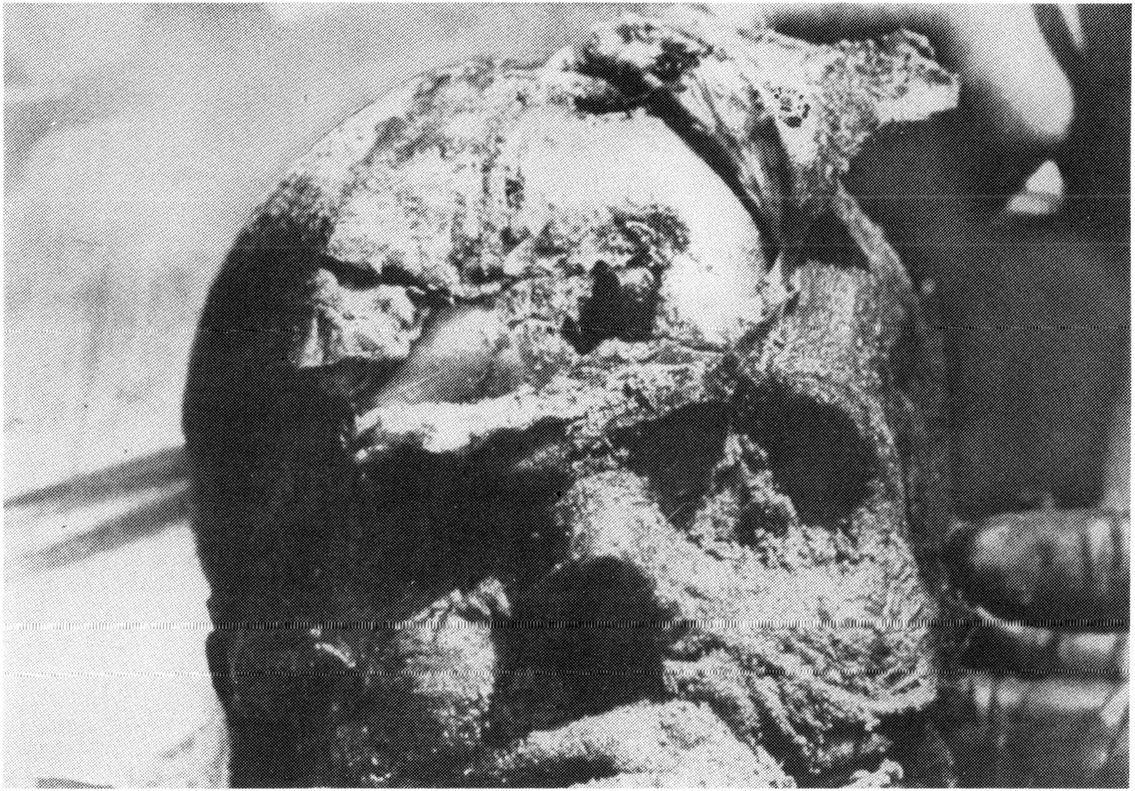

An diesem Schädel ist der Steckschuß deutlich zu erkennen, nur wenige Schädel weisen zwei bis drei Schüsse auf

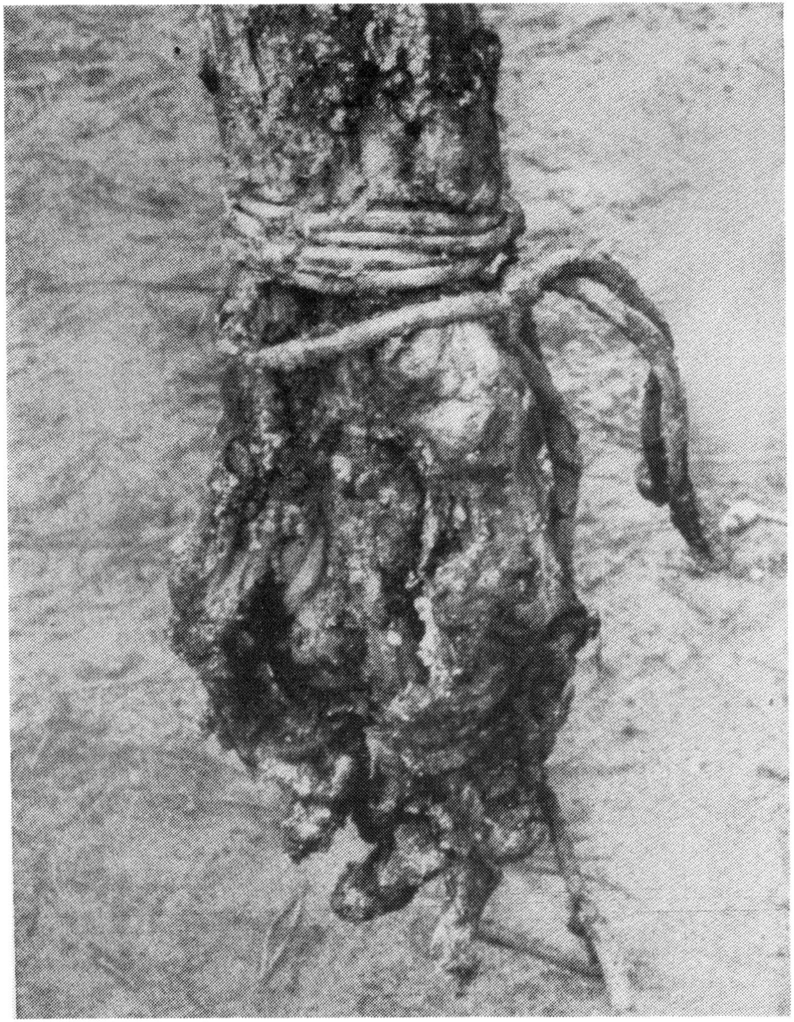

Stricke an den Händen vieler Leichen beweisen daß ein Teil der Opfer vor der Ermordung gefesselt wurde

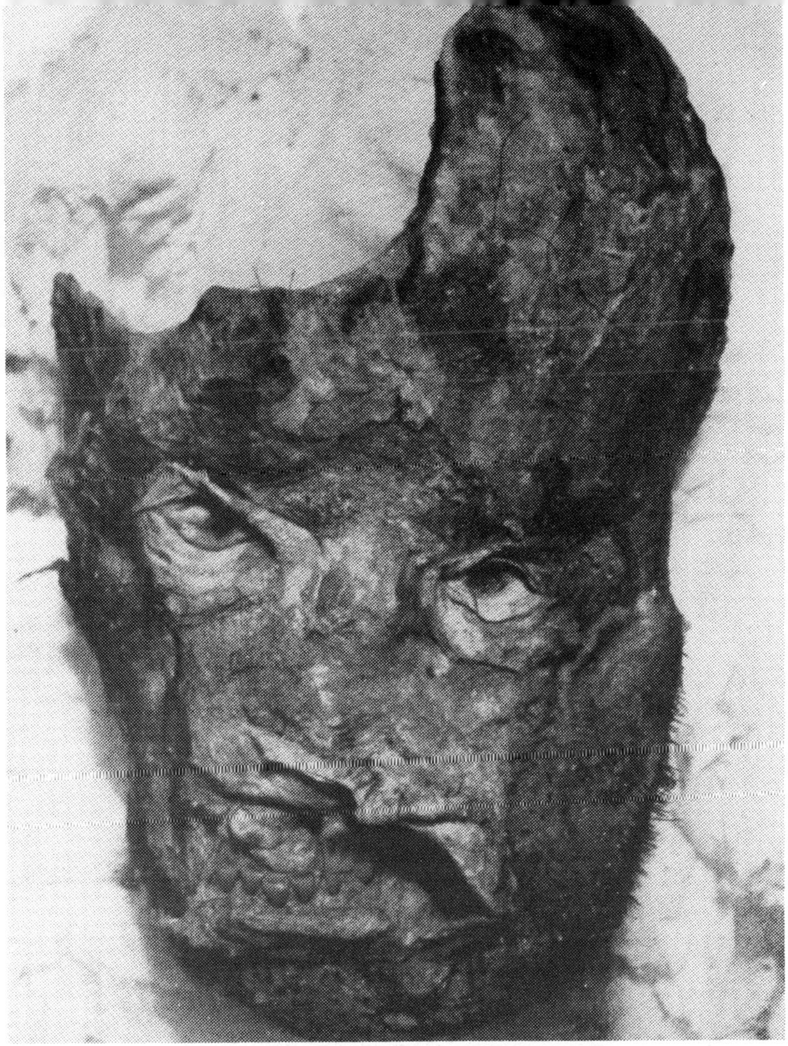

Grauenhaft verzerrt spiegelt dieser furchtbar verstümmelte Schädel die Qual der letzten Sekunden vor dem Morde wider

Mit Hilfe der einheimischen Bevölkerung, die sich freiwillig zur Verfügung stellte, wird Leiche auf Leiche aus den Gruben entfernt

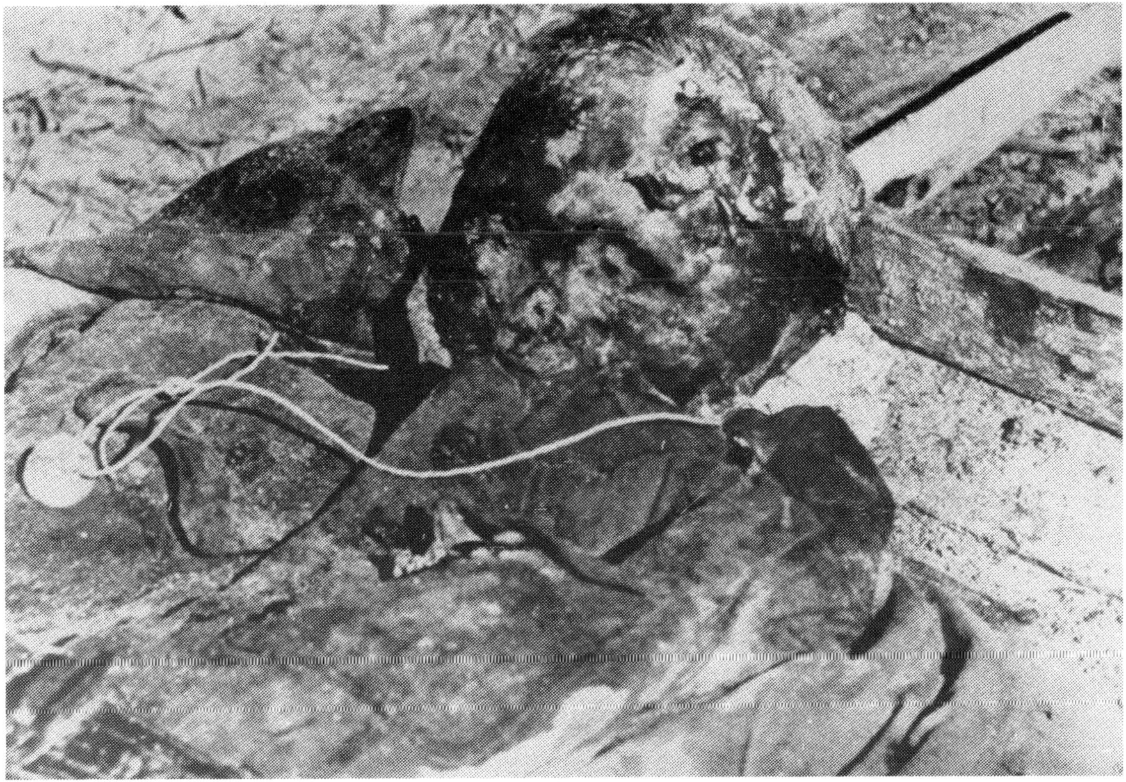

Zur Erleichterung der Obduktionsarbeiten wurden die identifizierten Leichen mit Erkennungsmarken versehen. Diese Überreste der Leiche des Brigadegenerals Smorawinski zeigen deutlich den Kopfsteckschuß; das Geschoß in der Schädeldecke ist noch sichtbar

Bei einer Leiche werden vor der endgültigen Bestattung die auf dem Rücken gefesselten Hände freigemacht

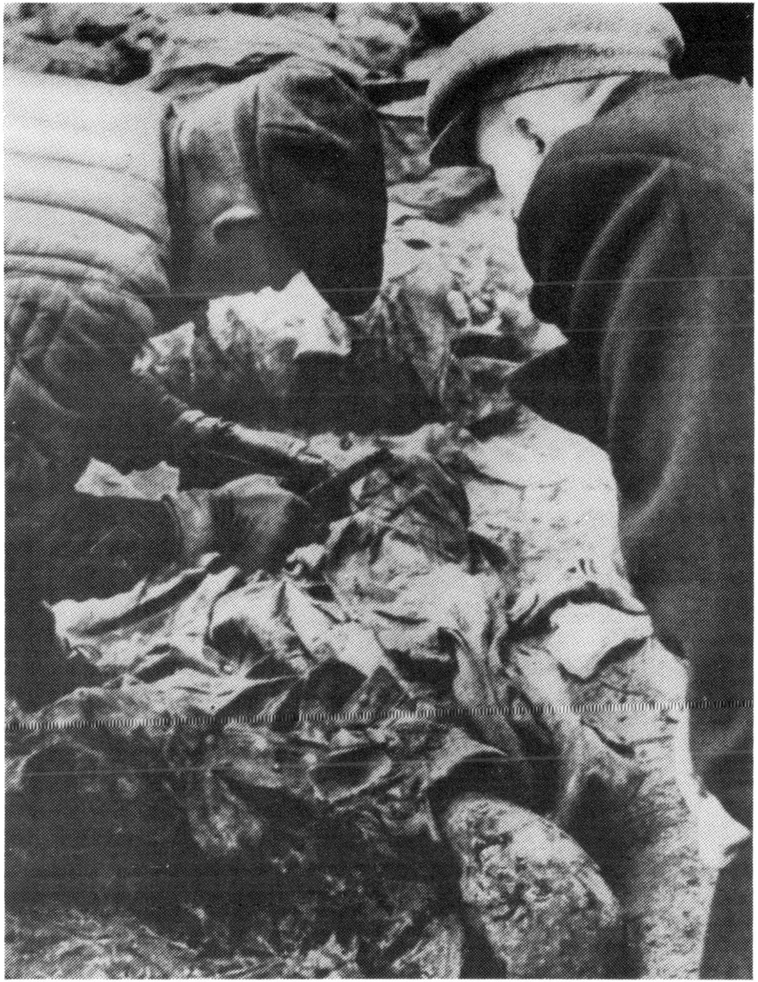

Gewissenhaft und sorgfältig wird jede einzelne Leiche untersucht. So konnten die Namen von rund 70 v. H. der Ermordeten festgestellt werden

Zahlreiche Bauern und Arbeiter aus der Umgebung des Mordwaldes, die die Transporte der polnischen Offiziere gesehen und die Schüsse gehört hatten, meldeten sich freiwillig als Zeugen

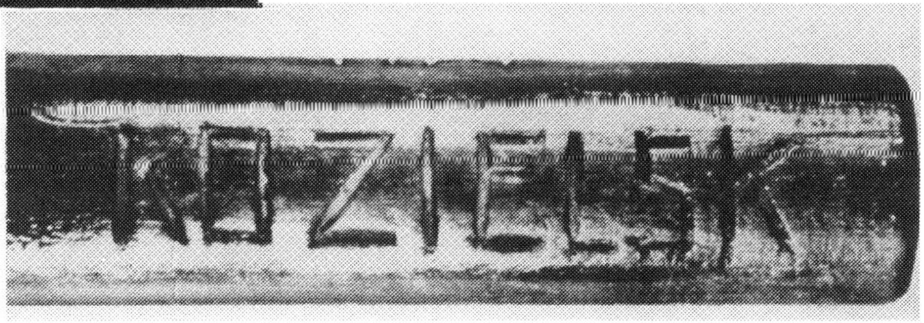

Ein hölzernes Zigarettenetui und eine Zigarettenspitze, die sich ein Gefangener im Lager von Kozielsk schnitzte. Alle wertvollen Schmuckgegenstände hatten die GPU-Henker ihren Opfern vor der Ermordung geraubt

Aus dem Tagebuch des polnischen Majors S o l s k i

(Leiche Nr. 0490)

8.4. 3.30 Uhr Ausfahrt aus der Station Kozielsk nach Westen. 9.45 Jelnia Station. Von 12 stehen wir auf dem Nebengleis.

9.4. Einige Minuten vor 5 Uhr früh werden wir geweckt und zum Verladen verteilt. Wir sollen auf Autos weggebracht werden. Was weiter?

9.4. um 5 Uhr früh. Von Tagesgrauen an beginnt der Tag nicht gut. Wir sind in Gefängwiswagen verladen. In den Abteilen Wache. Wir kommen in einen Wald – eine Art ~~Erholungshei~~ Sommererholungsheim. Gründliche Absuchung ...... Uhr, auf der die Zeit 6.30 oder (8.30) verzeichnet war. Sie fragen nach Trauringen. Sie nehmen ab Rubel, Hauptpass, Taschenmesser.

Ein erschütterndes Dokument: Die Übersetzung der letzten Seite aus dem Tagebuch des Majors Solski: „Wir kommen in einen Wald ...“

NR 2948

GENERALNY INSPEKTOR SIŁ ZBROJNYCH

KAPITUŁY ORDERU WOJENNEGO

„VIRTUTI MILITARI"

STWIERDZA, ŻE P. Mieczysław Smorawiński

JEST KAWALEREM KRZYŻA SREBRNEGO ORDERU WOJENNEGO „VIRTUTI MILITARI"

SZEF BIURA KAPITUŁY

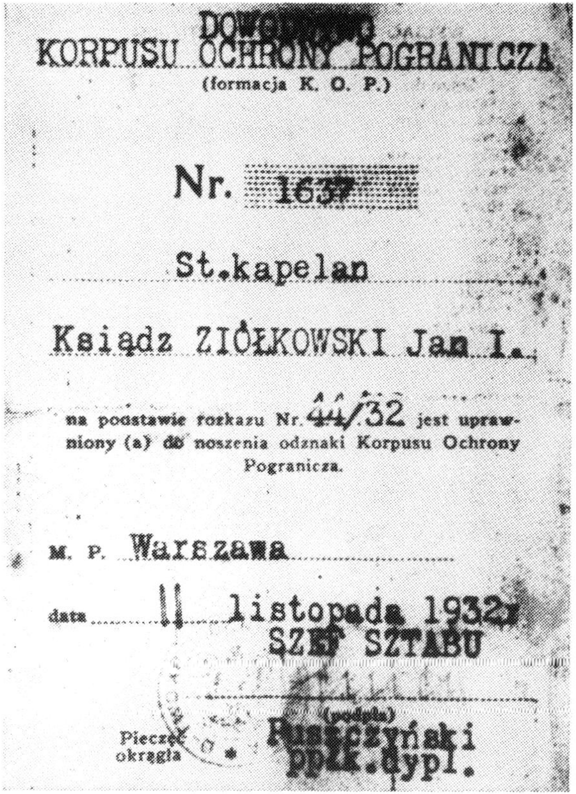

DOWÓDZTWO KORPUSU OCHRONY POGRANICZA
(formacja K. O. P.)

Nr. 1637

St.kapelan

Ksiądz ZIÓŁKOWSKI Jan I.

na podstawie rozkazu Nr. 44/32 jest uprawniony (a) do noszenia odznaki Korpusu Ochrony Pogranicza.

M. P. Warszawa

data 11 listopada 1932r.

SZEF SZTABU

(podpis)

Pieczęć okrągła

Ruszczyński
ppłk.dypl.

Solche für die Bolschewisten wertlosen Dokumente: Das Besitzzeugnis Nr. 2948 für die Tapferkeitsmedaille des Silbernen Kriegskreuzes „Virtuti Militari" des Generals Smorawinski Mieczyslaw und die Legitimation des Militärkaplans Jan Ziolkowski fand man bei zahlreichen Ermordeten

Die internationale Kommission von Gerichtsmedizinern aus allen Ländern Europas untersucht an langen Tischen die Leichen. Nichts wird unterlassen, ihre Identität festzustellen und den Angehörigen Nachricht zu geben

Die Stätte des Massenmordes von Katyn wurde Vertretern der gesamten europäischen Öffentlichkeit zugänglich gemacht. Zahlreiche Besucher, Pressevertreter und Angehörige des Roten Kreuzes vor allem, hatten Gelegenheit, die Stätte der bolschewistischen Bluttat zu besichtigen

Ehemalige polnische Soldaten besuchen den Tatort. Manch einer von ihnen erhielt hier Gewißheit von dem Tode seines früheren Kameraden

Translation continued.

exhibited distinguishing Polish characteristics such as buttons, insignia of service rank, decorations, military boots, laundry labels, etc. It is all winter clothing: furs, leather jackets, sweaters, heavy boots and typical Polish hats. Only a few of the corpses were not officers - one of them was a clergyman. The sizes of the clothing was consistent with the sizes of the bodies it was found on. Underwear was buttoned in an orderly way, suspenders and belts fastened as usual. From that it was concluded that the uniforms were being worn at the time of death and burial.

No watches or rings were found on the bodies, although watches must have been present around the time of death as detailed times were found in notes in dairies. Precious metals were found only in hidden places on a few corpses, but many corpses still had gold teeth. Lots of Polish bank notes were found along with a substantial amount of small change. Also found were packages of Polish cigarettes and matches. A few boxes of tobacco and cigarette holders were found engraved with the word “Kocielsk” (the name of the last Soviet prison camp of the victims). Documents found with the corpses (diaries, correspondence, newspapers) all dated from the fall of 1939 through March and April 1940. The last noted date is that on a Russian newspaper of 22 April 1940.

Different levels of decomposition among the corpses were noted. The level of decomposition depended upon where in the grave the body was taken from. The bodies found on top and on the sides of the mass graves were mummified, whereas bodies taken from the middle of the graves were still moist. Many corpses were stuck together by thickened body fluids. Deformation of many corpses resulted from the pressure exerted by the weight of the carefully arranged bodies above. None of the bodies showed any signs of insects or remains of insects that could date from the time of the burial. Noting this it was concluded that the executions and burials had to have taken place during a cold, insect-free time of year.

A large row of skulls were checked for irregularities. This was very important for Dr. Orsós to try to estimate the time of death. The skulls had a multi-layered volcanic limestone incrustation on the top side of the loamy homogenized brain mash below. The appearance of this combination will not be found in corpses that have laid in a grave for less than three years. A very pronounced example of this combination was found in the skull of corpse number 526, located in the top layer of a large mass grave.

Recapitulation of the verdict

Seven mass grave sites of Polish officers in the forest of Katyn were researched by the Commission. 982 bodies were exhumed, partially autopsied and studied. Seventy percent have been identified.

The cause of death of all the victims was a shot in the nape of the neck. From eye witness reports and from correspondence, diaries and newspapers found with the bodies it is concluded that the shootings took place in the months of March and April 1940. We are all in complete agreement with the findings written in the transcript regarding the mass graves and the individual corpses of Polish officers. [12 signatures]

The Katyn chapter is closed. But it will live on as the largest and most brutal mass murder in history. It is an especially gruesome case of Jewish-Bolshevistic murder practice. The entire European cultural world continues to battle against a system that promotes mass murder as a part of the political process. The victims of Katyn are now united with the victims

in Lithuania, Latvia and Estonia and with the millions of dead humans that the Bolsheviks have on their conscience after 25 years of bloody rule. This matter requires a clear decision on the part of every responsible European. Katyn is a horrible if typical example of what Bolshevism would do to all of Europe with the silent support of England and America. If it was up to them and their Jewish executioners, they would push westward and flood the cultivated European countries. If that happens the mass grave of tomorrow will not be called Katyn, but Europe. **F.R.**

[END OF TRANSLATION]

TRANSLATION OF ORIGINAL PHOTO CAPTIONS

1) In the neighborhood of Smolensk lies the stage of the most horrible murders in world history: here around 12,000 Polish officers were butchered like animals by the hangmen of the Soviet Union.

2) Here they are, silent witnesses of Bolshevik blood thirstiness, and an awful indictment against the hangmen of the Soviet Union and the Soviet Government.

3) Painstakingly, grave by grave Katyn was opened up. The corpses of the murdered officers were buried up to 4 meters deep.

4) A half opened pit: the skulls that are sticking out clearly show that the murder victims were piled up on top of each other.

5) This skull clearly shows the shot in the nape of the neck that all officers fell victim to.

6) The victims were found layered in several rows.

7) The mass graves of Katyn provide the world proof of the Bolshevik "love for mankind".

8) The length of the numerous graves in which the hangmen of the Soviet Union buried their victims was usually 15 x 30 meters.

9) These uncovered corpses are a horrific document of Bolshevik bestiality.

10) While many corpses were carefully arranged in rows, other victims were just thrown in graves by the Soviet butchers.

11) An awful sight: with hands tied and a bag over the head, this corpse was found in one of the pits.

12) The killing shots were fired from close range: besides an entry wound most skulls also show an exit at the top of the skull.

13) This skull clearly shows the retained bullet, only a few skulls proved to have 2 or 3 shots.

14) Bound hands on many corpses prove that part of the victims were tied up prior to being murdered.

15) Ghastly and distorted, this awfully mutilated skull mirrors the agony of the last minutes before the murders.

16) With help of volunteers from the local population, corpse after corpse was exhumed from the graves.

17) The identified bodies received ID tags to facilitate autopsies. The remains of the corpse of Brigadier General Smarowinski clearly shows the retained bullet, still visible in the skull.

18) Before the final burial, the hands that were tied behind the back of one of the corpses were undone.

19) Every single corpse was scientifically and carefully examined. As a result the names of about 70% of the victims could be established.

20) Many farmers and workers from the area of the murder site, who had seen the transports of Polish officers and heard the shots, volunteered as witnesses.

21) A wooden cigarette case and a cigarette holder carved by a prisoner of the Kozielsk camp. The Soviet hangmen robbed their victims of all valuables prior to their murders.

22) A shocking document: the translation of the last page from the diary of Major Solski: we are entering a forest...

23) These kinds of documents, valueless to the Bolsheviks, were found with many murder victims: certificate of ownership #2948 for the Silver War Cross "Virtuti Militari". It was a medal of bravery belonging to General Smorawinski Mieczyslaw; also the identification card of military chaplain Jan Ziolkowski.

24) The International Commission of doctors of forensic medicine from many countries in Europe examine corpses on long tables. Everything is done to establish their identity and to notify their next of kin.

25) The site of the mass murders of Katyn is accessible to representatives of the European public. Many visitors, press representatives and especially members of the Red Cross, had the possibility to view the site of this bloody Bolshevik deed.

26) Former Polish soldiers visit the scene of the crime. Many of them found out for sure about the death of their old comrades.

[END OF PHOTO CAPTION TRANSLATION]

By carefully tearing out the two translation pages in the back of this booklet, the two translation pages in the front will also be removed, and the booklet will be returned to its original 1943 German format.

Library of Congress Cataloging in Publication Data
Northstar Books Division, USM, Inc.
International Standard Book Number (ISBN) 0-910667-43-8

Title: **KATYN, a Documentary Account of the Evidence**
First American Edition

1. HISTORY, World War II, Poland, Soviet Union, Germany.
2. MEDICAL SCIENCE, Poland, Soviet Union, Germany, World War II.

Printed in the United States of America.

98765432

DISTRIBUTED EXCLUSIVELY WORLDWIDE BY

USM Inc., PO Box 810, Lakeville, MN 55044-0810 USA
Fax: (612) 469-4928